# The Church That Had Too Much

by

**Anita Mathias**

ISBN: 978-1-84902-656-7

I dedicate this fable to the Christian communities

in which I learned much

and grew much:

Grace Covenant Presbyterian Church, Williamsburg, Virginia,

Williamsburg Community Chapel, Williamsburg, Virginia,

and St. Aldate's Church, Oxford, England

## The Church That Had Too Much

Once upon a time,

there was a church

that had too much.

Now the members of this church worked hard

with great rectitude, and they had a good reputation

with believer and townsman alike,

and the work of their hands was blessed,

and they grew very rich.

And when the members of the church saw each other,

they said, “Oh, we *must* have you over.”

And then those who heard this

smiled a tight little smile,

and said, “Yes, and *we* must too.”

And each went away sad,

because they knew it would probably never be.

For the pretty damask sofas were littered
with toy helicopters from Hamleys which really flew,
and dolls which laughed and wet themselves,
and handheld computers and Nintendo and their living rooms
had toy cars which moved and beeped,
and toy kitchens with ovens which lit up and almost cooked,
and intricate monster doll houses,
and if other little children came,
their children would cry if their toys were touched,
or, heaven forbid, broken.

And in the study,
the shelves overflowed
with books bought which had been read,
or had been meant to be read,
but interests had changed,
and besides, with the demands of life and maintenance,
there was simply no time to read.

And littered in the study,
were DVDs which had been watched once,
and probably never would be again;
grimly educational documentaries, still shrink-wrapped;
VHS cassettes, but the VCR was broken,
and audio cassettes and CDs listened to
just once, whose sound one no longer liked.

THE COMPLETE ARKANGEL SHAKESPEARE
38 FULLY - DRAMATIZED UNABRIDGED PLAYS ON CD
BY WILLIAM SHAKESPEARE
As You Like It
Windsor
RICHARD III
PERICLES
King Lear
ARKANGEL
SLUMDOG MILLIONAIRE
FRANÇOIS TRUFFAUT
THE FILMS
6 DVD SET
DANGEROUS BEAUTY
AMAZING GRACE
A HISTORY OF CHRISTIANITY
THE COMPLETE ARKANGEL SHAKESPEARE
POSSESSION
GREECE
DYNASTIES
EMPIRES
PBS HOME VIDEO
KES
THE ERIC ROHMER COLLECTION
THE 400 BLOWS
THE Shakespeare COLLECTION

And scattered lay iPod Shuffles,
unused because the kids now had iPod Touches
just because everyone else had them,
and then upgraded to the sleek
iPod Nano for the video camera,
and then an iPhone 4
and finally, an iPad to stand out,
be distinguished and the envy of their form,
in a way far more easily accomplished
by kids whose parents have more than enough
than by the hard slog of swooping up prizes
(though with a status just as hollow--
but better a cool kid than a geek!)

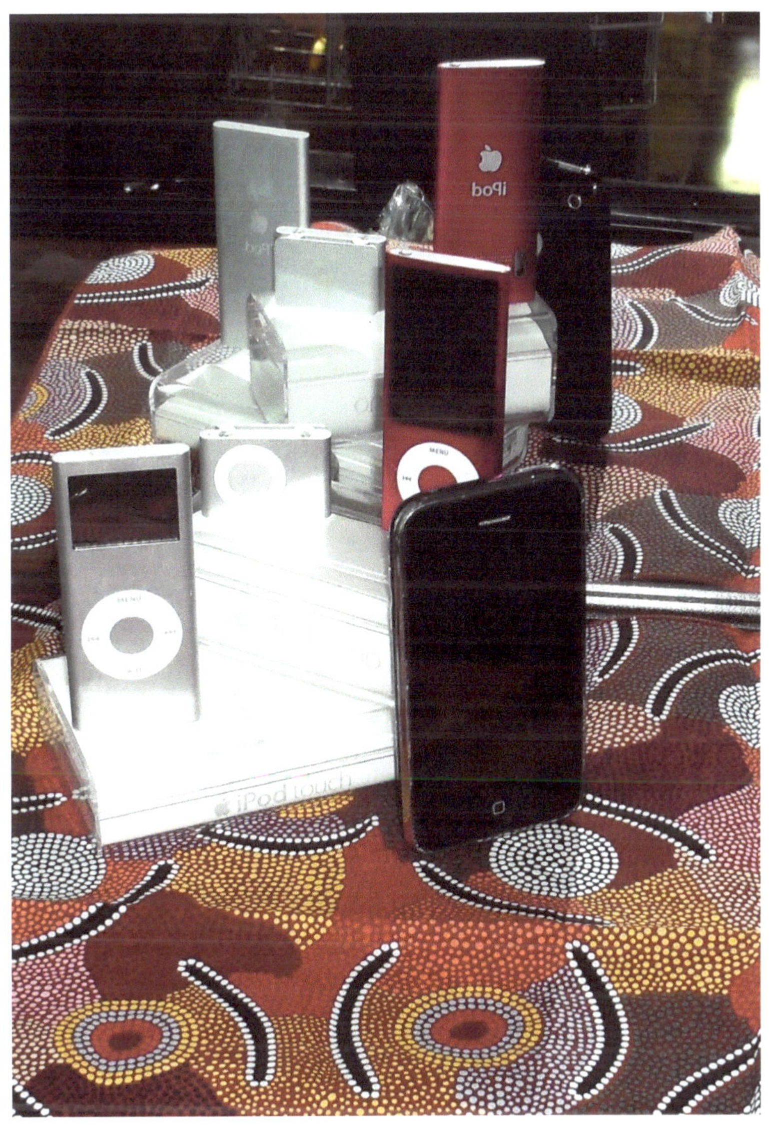
iPod touch

And in little piles lay
old mobile phones (wasn't there a charity
which recycled them?) and old laptops, ditto,
and coins in currencies no longer legal tender,
and gold watches which merely needed a new battery.

And in the kitchen,
the counters were cluttered--
visual stress, visual stress--
because the cabinets had ice cream makers and fondue sets,
and candy floss makers and chocolate fountains,
and the shelves were cluttered with
low fat cookbooks and French cookbooks,
and dessert cookbooks and Weight Watchers
and barbecue and vegetarian and Atkins cookbooks
and Indian, Thai, Chinese and Italian.

THE FOOD OF INDIA
THERE'S A CHEF IN MY SOUP!
PASTA, PIZZA, RISOTTO
RICE
classic vegetarian cooking
THE NEW BASICS COOKBOOK
Norman
SOUP BEAUTIFUL SOUP
Collins
THE COMPLETE BOOK OF NATURAL FOODS
SHAMBHALA
CHOOSE TO LOSE
WeightWatchers' New Complete Cookbook
THE New AMERICAN DIET
More-with-Less
REAL FAST FOOD
Simply in Season
THE 30-MINUTE COOK
NIGEL SLATER
CLASSIC SALADS
CHRISTINE INGRAM
KITCHEN LIBRARY
Baking
COOKERY BOOK
Recipes
THE ULTIMATE
COOKBOOK
THE PRACTICAL ENCYCLOPEDIA OF BAKING
THE TOP ONE HUNDRED PASTA SAUCES
Bittman
How to Cook Everything Vegetarian
Dr Atkins New Diet Revolution
FLAVOURED BREADS
smoothies
COMPLETE COOKERY COURSE

And then, just when you were nearly organised

Christmas came,

with sweaters and books and toys and games

there was simply no room to store

And if after a dozen “We must have you overs,”
you finally did,
you felt you should produce a meal worthy
of this protracted invitation,
and where could one find the energy to do that?

And guests meant stress,
stuffing stuff into closets
from which the stuffing fell out if they were opened,

And one couldn’t put them in the garage
which was cluttered with mulchers and jigsaws
and strimmers and shredders and mowers.

And at the end, just before your guests came,
you could never find anything to wear
because clothes, outgrown, or too expensive
to just give away, or too worn and stained to donate,
but not worn and stained enough to toss
cluttered the closets so that
the elegant clothes could never be found,
and you felt that you had simply nothing to wear
and so bought some more, which were somewhere,
(but where?) and were always late while you extricated
something which matched from your disorganised abundance.

* * *

Mrs. Hadenough had had enough and more than enough.

Her big house with its crystal, chandeliers and cuckoo clocks;

its antique furniture, original paintings,

*pietre dure* marble chests,

Murano paperweights and vases

brought her no peace,

but ruined her rest--

just brought her stress

because it was simply too much.

And when she went to her women's Bible study,
her friends talked about *things*--
things on sale, things on Freecycle,
things they had bought or wanted to buy,
and how busy and overwhelmed they were,
sorting out their houses full of things,
taking them to the charity shops
to make room for more things,
and about where to find nifty little organising boxes,
clothes boxes, tool boxes and craft boxes to store
the simply too many things.

And then she read what the Native Americans
of the Pacific Northwest did
when they had simply too much.

They had a potlatch,
grandly sharing their amassed possessions,
and then resumed their simple happy lives,
tidepooling on the Oregon Coast,
enjoying salmon, oysters, mussels and crab.

But how does one have a potlatch

like the North American Indians?

And in the bulletin that Sunday,
she put an announcement
about a kitchen gadget exchange.

The next Sunday, along with the tithe,
each family was to bring something
they never used: cappuccino makers
and coffee grinders in newly decaffeinated families;
yoghurt makers, omelette pans, electric spice graters,
asparagus or fish steamers to give and to take.

And when, after the service, impatient queues formed,
she was sad to spot the acquisitive eyes of the hunter,
when what she wanted to learn and teach was
that it is in giving that we receive.
She suggested that to force themselves to become givers,
people first offer what they really, really wanted
to a couple of others before taking it.

SWAN

And so, in a spirit of jollity, people offered
each other good gifts so that everyone
who, in a moment of folly,
had bought a ravioli maker or an oyster shucker
could now give it to those who always had wanted
a ravioli maker or an oyster shucker,
until they too passed it on.

And so everyone went home with something
they really wanted out of the community's abundance.

And then it was the turn of books.

Those who had bought *Money, Sex and Power,*

*The Freedom of Simplicity*, *The Mustard Seed Conspiracy,*

or *Rich Christians in an Age of Hunger*, but realised

that they made being simple no easier,

but being complex a guiltier undertaking

put them on the table, so that those who instinctively

began a new undertaking by reading a book

could get them for free.

And everyone went home smiling,

as they did on DVD Sunday.

And outgrown toys were shared,
so that every child had fascinating things to play with,
until they outgrew them,
and then, they swapped.

And lovely expensive clothes
which no longer fitted
could be swished with other people:
cashmere sweaters in the wrong colour
or just a little too tight or too loose,
and so when one's look changed
and one began to dress up or down or bright or old,
the change could bless someone else.

And so each Sunday, the congregation brought
a designated item along with the tithe,
blessing each other with their surplus,
and the church rented a storehouse for what wasn't taken.

And soon, people began to get rid of
a shirt saved for when they painted,
or scruffy shoes to wear if they gardened,
or Christian books to read when they had time,
because they could always pick them up from the storehouse.

And people began to go to the church's storehouse first,
instead of the shops (greatly helping their budgets!)
and eventually everyone had everything they really needed
and donated the rest to the storehouse,
decluttering until everything in their houses
was both beautiful and useful.

"If you want a golden rule that will fit everything, this is it: Have nothing in your houses that you do not know to be useful or believe to be beautiful."

William Morris

And once a month, the doors of the storehouse

were opened to the community:

You could bring your surplus, or take

other peoples', no strings or questions,

so that the church became known as The Giving Church.

And because there was always the storehouse,
where, in lean seasons, you could get the beans,
quinoa, amaranth and orzo your friends had bought
in fits of healthfulness, but never cooked,
or the electric saw or strimmer you needed once a year,
people no longer held onto everything
for fear they might one day need it,
or worried about their budgets quite so much
because in a pinch, you could get stationery,
clothes and food—most things you needed--from the storehouse.

And there were no poor among them.

And in the newly sleek houses,

hours of maintenance were released,

and people entertained their friends.

*Consider the Lilies*

And once letting go became a habit,
people discovered, to their surprise,
that they were valued for the content of their characters,
that people actually liked them
even when they no longer subtly showed off
about what they had or did.

And then, having happily shed so much,
they decided to shed a little more,
and Mrs Shortnplump forgave Mrs Tallnthin
who had manoeuvred the Bible study they co-led
out of her dreamy hands with Machiavellian whispers,
and back-stabbing worthy of a presidential campaign.
Mrs Tallandthin had won that power struggle,
and she had lost.
And so what?

In the Upside Kingdom, manipulators
did not inherit the reward of the meek,
and those who lost the world might gain their souls,
and, in mysterious ways, inherit the world besides.
And Mrs Brown forgave Mrs Black who, working
the vicar's wife and everyone else, swiped the leadership
of the Friday women's coffee group
(informally known as sit and bitch)
from her.  And so what?

And Mr. Doeverything decided that since he came home
at nine, after his children were in bed, he really
did not need to run the building programme too,
that he could shed his campaign to be Someone Very
Important in the very small world of the church
and instead spend his time with those he really loved.

And Mr. Ineverypie who was away from home for 99 days
each year, swallowed his pride, and resigned as Chair
of the Development Committee, letting go of the fear
that no one would know who he was, if he were not always
onstage (oh, they did, they did, they surely did!)
and instead rediscovered his delight in his wife
and littlest minx, whom he adored,
when he let his eyes linger on her.

And following their lead,

those who were ambitious to strut their stuff

slowly grew willing to wait for the "Friend, Come Higher,"

trusting their PR to God,

never seeking, never refusing, a position of greater influence.

And the church was no longer a seven storey mountain

of social ascent, and when they got together

people no longer reserved their warmest smiles

and shiniest manners for those at the top of the ant-heap,

as if one could absorb significance by association.

***He that is down needs fear no fall;***
***He that is low, no pride;***
***He that is humble ever shall***
***Have God to be his guide.***

*In The Valley of Humiliation, a man shall be free from the noise and from the hurryings of this life. All states are full of noise and confusion, only the Valley of Humiliation is that empty and solitary place. Here a man shall not be so let and hindered in this contemplation as in other places he is apt to be. This is a valley that no one walks in, but those that love a pilgrim's life. I must tell you that in former times men have met with angels here, have found pearls here, and have in this place found the words of life."* John Bunyan, *The Pilgrim's Progress*

They surrendered their longing to belong to
the church's inner circle: Those who knew who
was who, and what had happened,
was happening, and would happen,
and instead hung out with those they really liked,
and so in time formed their own inner circles,
not necessarily important ones in the eyes of the church
but just people who enjoyed being with each other.

And so everyone looked forward to social gatherings,
even fund-raisers, for they would get to relax
with those they loved being with,
instead of seeking out those
more important than themselves
who, in turn, looked restlessly around, scanning the crowd,
for someone still more important.

*I believe that in all men's lives at certain periods, and in many men's lives at all periods between infancy and extreme old age, one of the most dominant elements is the desire to be inside the local Ring and the terror of being left outside.*

*The quest of the Inner Ring will break your hearts unless you break it.*

*And if in your spare time you consort simply with the people you like, you will again find that you have come unawares to a real inside: that you are indeed snug and safe at the centre of something which, seen from without, would look exactly like an Inner Ring. But the difference is that it is only four or five people who like one another meeting to do things that they like. This is friendship. Aristotle placed it among the virtues. It causes perhaps half of all the happiness in the world, and no Inner Ringer can ever have it.*

"The Inner Ring" by C.S. Lewis

And when the church decided to close the storehouse,
because fewer and fewer people visited it,
since all had all they needed and had given away
all they did not, so that everything left in their houses
was both beautiful and useful,
people did not even notice,
for they now lived in the new way
of Content.

Letting go, letting go,
of everything they no longer needed,
blessing others with it,
and, in turn, being blessed
in the mysterious divine economy
no economist can fathom.

Letting go
of old grievances,
releasing people into the waterfall of grace,
letting God deal with them,
letting go of the desire to be a big deal,
remembering that they belonged to a Kingdom
which already had a King.

Pressing on, pressing on,

to know God more,

to love God more, and

to love people more.

And they were known as Christians by their love.

Acknowledgments

The Church That Had Too Much and its parishioners are a composite, and are not directly based on any church or individual, alive or dead.

I am grateful to my husband, Roy Mathias, and my daughter Zoe Mathias for handling the illustrations—a task entirely beyond me, and to my friends Ruth French, Jo Mitchell and Susan Griffith for their careful and astute readings.

About the Author

Anita Mathias is the author of *Wandering Between Two Worlds: Essays on Faith and Art.* She has a B.A. and M.A. in English from Somerville College, Oxford University, and an M.A. in Creative Writing from the Ohio State University, USA. Anita won a National Endowment of the Arts fellowship in Creative Nonfiction in 1997. She lives in Oxford, England with her husband, Roy, and her daughters, Zoe and Irene.

Visit Anita at http://www.anitamathias.com, and on http://theoxfordchristian.blogspot.com, her Christian blog; http://wanderingbetweentwoworlds.blogspot.com/, her personal blog, and http://thegoodbooksblog.blogspot.com, her literary and writing blog.